Perth Memories

Once upon a time, Perth was the capital of Scotland and a picturesque playground for kings and queens. Today, the city is laced with gorgeous architecture, unrivalled surrounding landscapes and an intriguing royal history.

The charm of every great city lies in its people, culture and traditions. And Perth has all of these in spades. This fascinating collection of recently discovered archive photographs features Perth – and its proud inhabitants – from decades gone by. Lovingly restored, these images shed light on the history of one of our most fascinating cities.

A day at the races - as the crowd gathered for the spring meeting of the Perth Hunt in April 1975.

The horses and jockeys in the paddock before the start of the fourth race at Perth Hunt meeting at Scone in October 1978.

The enclosure was at full capacity for the National Hunt meeting which took place at Scone in September 1977.

Enjoying the lovely weather in the owners and trainers enclosure at the National Hunt in September 1979.

Poly Boy racing to the finish line at the Black Watch Selling Handicap Hurdle Race in April 1975.

Scone Palace, one of the finest examples of Georgian Gothic style in the UK.

Spring arrived at Scone Palace in April 1987.

Visitors enjoying the sunshine outside the chapel of Scone Palace in September 1980.

9

Looking over Smeaton's Bridge towards the North Inch in this scenic image from March 1968.

Looking towards Rose Terrace from North Inch in March 1979.

Charlotte Street with North Inch and Smeaton's Bridge on the left in August 1954.

North Inch with the Prince Albert Monument on right and Charlotte Place on left in September 1961.

The Fourth Royal Tank Regiment brought along their Scorpion and Fox armoured vehicles for a demonstration which was held at North Inch in September 1978.

The gathering of The 51st Highland Division reunion which was held at North Inch in October 1963.

Playing and skating on the ice at a time when the River Tay had completely frozen over.

The sun was shining at a busy open market at Muirton Park in May 1975.

This stallholder held the crowd's attention at his stall selling bedding at the open market at Muirton Park in 1975.

These ladies are looking through some of the curtain material for sale at the open market in Muirton Park in 1975.

Everyone was looking to grab a bargain at the first Open Air Market to be held at Muirton Car Park for some years in May 1975.

Pullars Dyeworks building on Kinnoull Street was the largest dyeworks in Scotland in the late 19th century.

Matthew Gloag & Son Ltd wine merchants on Kinnoull Street in March 1980.

The newly-opened Presto Supermarket on Kinnoull Street in October 1980.

Sandeman Library on the corner of Mill Street and Kinnoull Street in 1947.

This wonderful view of Tay Street was captured from across the river in June 1969.

Buying or just browsing, there was something for everyone to enjoy at the 'Art Mart' sale of artworks on Tay Street in May 1976

Not everyone was interested in art at the Festival of Arts which took place on Tay Street in May 1975.

Art sale on the banks of the Tay in May 1978.

Looking over the river
towards the Fair City in 1976.

The Court House and spire of St Matthew's Church on Tay Street in 1955.

Tay Street with the Court House and St Matthew's Church in 1949.

The sun is shining on a snow-covered Tay Street in February 1978.

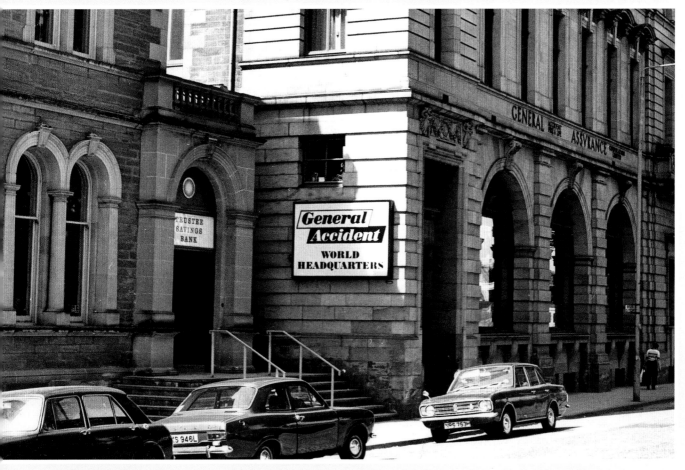

The World Headquarters of General Accident on Tay Street in 1977.

Lady Georgina Home Drummond laying the foundation stone of the General Accident Assurance Co. Ltd. premises on the site of the old Post Office in Tay Street in July 1899.

General Accident Assurance Co. Ltd. building on the High Street as it was in September 1958.

A view of the High Street as it was in April 1956.

Policeman directing traffic on the High Street in 1956.

Bruce's Record Shop and the Skirt N Slack Centre can be seen on the left-hand side of the High Street in June 1974.

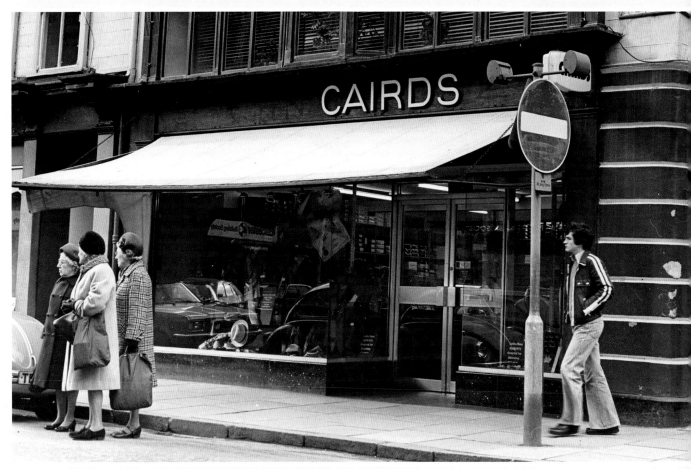

Cairds clothing store on the High Street in March 1978.

Marks & Spencer was attracting attention to passers-by prior to opening in November 1962.

The High Street was much brighter in 1977 as new Christmas lights had been purchased.

Making a dash, while the traffic had stopped at the junction of High Street and South Street.

Abbey National and John Menzies can be seen on the left and True Form shoe shop on the right of the High Street in May 1977.

The High Street taken from St Paul's Church in May 1966.

Window shopping on the High Street at Charles Rattray tobacconist in December 1980.

If you were looking to purchase household items then Frank Thomson in the High Street was the place to go in 1962.

The archaeological excavation which took place in the High Street between 1975 and 1977 revealed many thousands of items relating to daily life in 14th century Perth.

Another shot of the archaeological excavation which took place in November 1975.

The first guided tour of the Scottish Parliament excavation site in High Street, which took place a week ahead of schedule in February 1976.

Perth Museum and Art Gallery on George Street in 1953.

Perth Art Gallery and Museum in November 1976.

This image showcases the distinctive domed roof and pillars of the Museum and Art Gallery in June 1947.

Exterior of the old City Hall, with people gathered around the cobbled square in 1938.

Looking over towards King Edward Street from the High Street in April 1939.

King Edward Street in September 1961.

49

The opening ceremony of St John's Square shopping centre in July 1961.

St John's Square in 1961 featuring a sign for Marks & Spencer which was due to open in November the following year.

St John's Square as it was in July 1961 before the shopping centre was built.

These ladies were ready to shop as they stepped into St John's Square in June 1975.

Stopping for a break while out shopping at St John's Square in May 1963.

McEwens on St John Street in December 1966.

Glens of Perth Ltd department store on St John Street in October 1962.

Laing & Co. delicatessen and wine shop on the right of St John Street in May 1966.

St John's Kirk on St John's place in 1951.

Looking down St John Street towards the High Street in October 1962.

Victoria Bridge was built in 1900 to provide a second crossing and was replaced by Queen's Bridge in 1960.

The opening ceremony of the new Queen's Bridge, by Her Majesty Queen Elizabeth II, on October 10, 1960.

Queen Elizabeth II inspecting the troops during the opening ceremony of the Queen's Bridge.

The Queen accepting a gift on the newly opened Queen's Bridge.

The Queen inspecting police officers during her visit to the city.

Queen's Bridge, looking over towards Dundee Road in 1968.

A busy South Street looking towards Dundee Road in May 1963.

Brydens Indoor Market on South Street in April 1980.

Looking on to Watergate from South Street in March 1964.

Looking towards MacPherson Groceries on South Street in 1950.

The Courier was delivering the latest news to R. Campbell grocery and provisions in South Street in 1950.

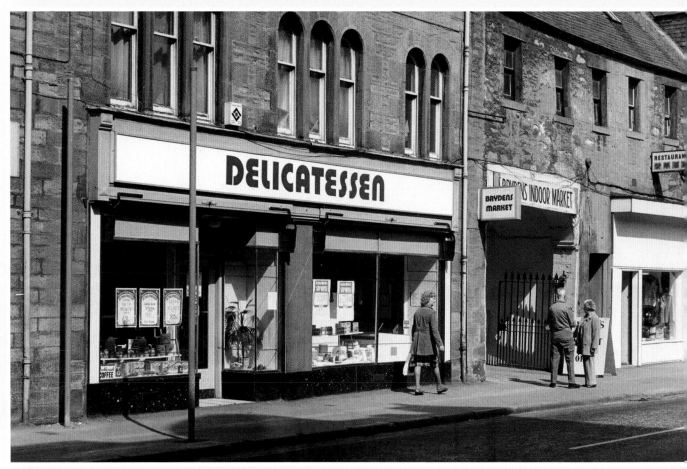

Brydens Indoor Market on South Street in April 1980.

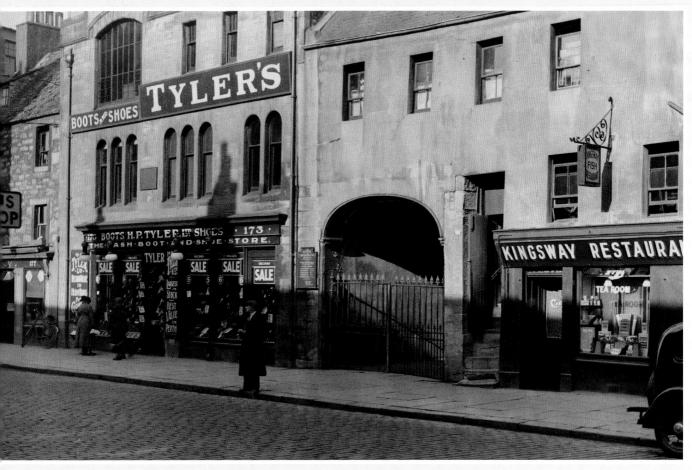

The entrance to the original Secession Church on South Street in February 1937.

James G. Falls grocery store on the corner of Hospital Street and County Place in September 1961.

The Meal Vennel before it was demolished to make way for the present St John's Square.

A rooftop view of the tower above the railway station in April 1959.

The bus stance outside Perth Railway Station in October 1961.

Perth Railway Station, with the Station Hotel on the right and the bus stance in the foreground in October 1961.

A crowd gathered to watch the opening of the newly-built Pomarium Street multi-storey flats in March 1960.

The living room of one of the newly-built flats in Pomarium Street in April 1960.

A sneak peek into a freshly-decorated bedroom of one of the Pomarium Street flats in April 1960.

Cars carefully negotiating the snow-covered road on Tay Street in February 1978.

McLaughlan Brothers on Canal Street in September 1978.

There was a delivery of Pepsi-Cola to the Pavilion Transport Cafe on Princes Street in June 1969.

Looking along Princes Street in 1966.

Frew & Company Ltd Garage on Princes Street, with several cars parked in and around it, in 1922.

Looking along Marshall Place with St Leonard's-in-the-Fields Church on the left and the Sir Walter Scott monument on the rig

The rotunda pictured here in 1953 was the city's first waterworks when it was built in 1832 and remained as a pumping station until 1965.

Casting a reflection on peaceful
waters in the harbour in 1948.

Boats docked in the lower harbour in January 1971.

Magula, is pictured here at the harbour, where it was being loaded with timber to be shipped to Sweden in February 1978

Men were at work on board the Hullgate as it was docked at the harbour in 1954.

The Spring Lass being loaded with barley for transport to the continent in December 1980.

The Krasnal was the third largest ship to dock in the harbour in February 1972.

The harbour was undergoing renovation in 1955 - photo shows a pile driver replacing metal sides to the wall.

McLennan Marine shop in the harbour which produced and supplied all types of small craft in February 1971.

The harbour was frozen over in the winter of 1963.

An aerial view of the harbour captured in 1988.

Children playing as people take a stroll around South Inch in 1947.

Large crowds attended the Agricultural Show which was held at South Inch in August 1979.

The Harness Section at the Agriculture Show, South Inch in August 1972.

This gentleman travelled around the Argricultural Show in style in 1978.

The Jubliee May Fayre attracted the crowds when it was held at South Inch in 1977.

There was a long queue for refreshments.

Preparation was under way to create a garden for the blind in South Inch in August 1957, with the plan to plant strongly scented flowers and erect a plaque in braille which would describe them.

This hot air balloon was about to take off from the South Inch in June 1977 – the balloon was brought in to publicise Perth Theatre's 'Summer Scotch 77'.

The children of Letham Kirk attended the 1977 May Fayre held by Perth Round Table and Ladies Circle at South Inch in fancy dress. The costumes based on the nursery rhyme 'There was an Old Lady who lived in a Shoe'.

Children were trying their hands at rowing on the boating pond during the Easter holiday in April 1979.

Enjoying a day out on the boats at South Inch Pond in April 1957.

Everyone enjoyed the lovely summer holiday
weather in 1977 around the pond at South Inch.